How to Do...

an Image Consult

10 Steps to Fashion & Style Transformation

By Gillian Armour, AICI CIP

First Printing, March 2010
Volume II November 2010
10 9 8 7 6 5 4 3 2 1

ISBN 1456450441
EAN-13 9781456450441

Printed in the United States of America.
Set in Calibri.

Images used with permission: Microsoft, Gillian Armour, istock and Image Works.

• • •

INTRODUCTION

I wrote this guide to a professional image consult based on my years of experience with hundreds of clients. The first years of practicing as a professional image consultant were hit and miss. I did not have a guide such as this one to help me along. Everything you read here is synthesized from my personal and professional experiences. Hopefully by sharing my experiences I can save you a great deal of time and energy.

Over the years I have added many services onto my menu of options for clients. You will find yourself doing the same as you gain in experience and build your client base.

The following guidelines take you through the ten simple steps of an image makeover. My method is based on the transformative steps I take my clients through. I have edited this guide down to 10 simple steps you need to take to complete a thorough consultation. Obviously you can add or subtract services as you see fit.

Before beginning your work with the client, know the journey, and the steps you will be taking with her by focusing on the services you will be offering. You will also need to review her needs, why she is hiring you. Once you have an idea of her needs you can then talk about the various services you offer. Here are a few examples:

Full image makeover – typically for a client in need of a major overhaul. New personal image, new clothes, coaching for non-verbal skills, hairstyle analysis, color analysis and a shopping trip. This session can take up to four hours.

Makeover – for the client who needs advice about what to wear and how to wear it. A typical session takes two hours.

Color Analysis – this client just wants to know what her best colors are.

Personal Shopping Trip – established clients will repeat this service with you many times.

Body Shape Analysis – using the forms in this book, you can determine both a clients horizontal and vertical body shape.

The following principles and commitments are my personal and professional credo, or statement of belief. My credo is based on the book **Consulting Mastery: How the Best Make the Biggest Difference**, by Keith Merron. This book had a huge impact on me when, after many years of practicing these standards on my own, I read Merron's book and recognized his descriptions of how to work with clients as the same standards I had been practicing my entire career. You may want to customize a credo of your own similar to this one and review it with clients *before* you begin your work together:

THE MASTER IMAGE CONSULTANTS CREDO

PRINCIPLES AND COMMITMENTS BETWEEN YOU AND YOUR CLIENT

- I am committed to your success.
- I tell the truth and expect you to do the same.
- I act with integrity and expect you to do the same.
- I will help you make your vision a reality.
- I create images and tell stories through styling; your job is to give me your story.
- All of our interactions and transactions are confidential.
- I offer you the best service levels and you offer me gratitude when our work together is well done.

_____

Agreed to by / date

STEP 1 - CLIENT INTERVIEW

It's important to know everything there is to know about your client. We have supplied samples of forms you can use. (Find these forms on page 15).

1) **Client Application**
2) **Client Needs Analysis**
3) **Image Consultation Survey**
4) **Personal Style Questionnaire**
5) **Creative Fashion Profile**
6) **Non-verbal Communication Review**

The initial interview is a great time for you to befriend the client. Of course, you should always keep your relationship professional, but as an image consultant you will need to know intimate details about your client (her weight, measurements, likes, frustrations, shopping habits and personal taste to name just a few). Your people skills will come in handy during this initial stage of the relationship.

Begin your sessions with clients by focusing on the task at hand – them. They may be hiring you to polish their image, to help them land a job, or to get them a date! But most of the time your personal clients will want one thing only – to look and feel great with your help.

During the initial interview with your client (use the questionnaires in this chapter) it helps to discuss such things as:

- Their lifestyle – leisure activities, travel, social life, etc.

- What they do for fun – dinner out, gallery walks, museum tours, etc.

- Why do they need your help?

- When will they need your help?

- What upcoming appearances, events, jobs, and social occasions will they need you for? Use your calendar and start taking note of the dates they give you.

- List their favorite clothing designers.

- Ask about personal tastes, likes, dislikes about fashion, art, style, etc.

- Take measurements (if applicable to the project) and define body shape.

- Use form supplied to detail any wardrobe plans or needs they have.

- Make a shopping list.

Now that you have completed your initial interview with your client you can move on to the second part of the client interview process (either continue or reschedule).

Bring out "clarify" their vision

The most important part of starting any new project with a potential client is to get clear (on the same page, if you will) about their vision for what they want to accomplish. Frequently your clients will not be able to give you an exact idea therefore it is your job to illicit information from them by asking questions, lots of questions. Your goal is to get the best picture of their vision so you can deliver on the dream. As you gain experience in this process you will develop your own way of crafting and forming your client's visions. Below are a few questions I ask my clients.

- Tell me how you see yourself at the end of our work together.

- What is your vision for yourself (for the project)?

- What kind of research do we need to do?

- What kind of background information can you give me that will help me create a successful look, project, end result?

- If you had to pull references what would they be? Fashion history, fashion designers, celebrity looks?

- Give me some personal history that will help me understand who you are as a person.

- Brainstorm session – you can draw pictures with client of ideas they have, do a collage of cutouts from magazines, start a story board with them.

Based on all the above information you gather, tell them what you think the picture of them (or the picture of the project) is starting to look like. Do not give them all the details. You will flesh out ideas later on, in your own time, and will use your own method of storyboarding, scrap booking or look-books.

Before and After

Discover and detail their budget (ask lots of questions, take lots of notes)

The best time to discuss costs and budgets with clients is within the first interview. Most clients have a very good idea of how much they want to spend with you. Sometimes they are way off and need to be gently brought back to reality. Because financial matters are sensitive you must always, always write the details down. Even before you work up a formal budget presentation for the client you will be making notes of what you discuss when it comes to money. Whether your client is an individual or a business, financial details are important. Financial communication is at the top of the list of successful budget controls. Your clients will want to have an open and honest relationship with you about their budgetary concerns, limitations, abilities etc.

- Start by asking them what their projected expenditure/ budget is.

- Have they thought about the details of the project and the costs involved in accomplishing their vision?

- In how much time do they expect to have the project completed?

- Do they want full service packages (full image makeover, shopping trips and spa service) or just menu items (such as color analysis, body shape and measurements)?

- When it comes to shopping for them ask if they want you to consult with them before you buy anything.

- Discuss how you will be reimbursed if you do shop for them.

CLIENT APPLICATION

NAME:

ADDRESS:

CITY / STATE/ ZIP

CELL PHONE:_____ **HOME PHONE:**_____

EMAIL ADDRESS_____

What is your profession?

How did you hear about _____ Image Consulting?

Why are you here today?   Fee discussed?

Please write a few words about how you are presenting yourself to the outside world through your appearance. *Add commentary to this description based on what you think others would say about your look.*

(Example: I wear a lot of black and I think that makes me look severe.)

Why do you think you need image-related services?

Have you ever had a makeover before?

Are you in need of our services for a specific event? Explain.

Do you have special physical needs that make it hard for you to wear certain things? (e.g.: I have fallen arches so I can't wear heels.)

Do you want supporting consultations for etiquette, voice, mannerism awareness or visual poise?

What do you think an Image Consultant can do for you?

What do you hope to have learned at the end of your personal consultation?

IMAGE CONSULTATION SURVEY

Circle each answer that applies:

APPEARANCE

1. I need to update my appearance
2. I'd like to know what's in fashion
3. I don't know my body type
4. I want to raise my self-confidence
5. I want a complete change of style
6. I'd like a new hairstyle
7. I need advice about makeup
8. I need advice about grooming
9. I want to know what colors look best on me
10. I would like to know how to dress/ coordinate
11. I want to learn about fabrics and care of clothes

SELF IMAGE

12. I'd like to know how my appearance affects others
13. I want my self-esteem raised
14. My body has changed and I'd like to know how to wear flattering styles
15. I want to look great all the time
16. I want others to take me seriously
17. I need to appear professional and in control

PERSONAL/ PROFESSIONAL DEVELOPMENT

18. I want to know how to organize my closet
19. I'd like to have an expert show me how to dress for more success
20. I want to build my wardrobe around classic styles
21. I'd like to stop wasting money on clothes that I never wear
22. I'd like to know more about etiquette
23. I want to feel I can fit in anywhere
24. I want to improve my social skills
25. I need help with my manners
26. I want to improve my speaking skills

What is the story you would like to tell about yourself? How can that story be told through your image?

PERSONAL STYLE QUESTIONNAIRE for_____

Please provide as much information as you can when answering the following questions. Your answers will help determine a plan for creating your **personal style** and developing **image confidence**.

1. How would you describe your current image?

2. How would you describe your **ideal** image?

3. How would you describe your personality?

4. Whose personal style do you admire and why?

5. What does a typical day involve for you?

How do you feel about your….

Personal Style?	Excellent	Fair	Below Average
Fashion Awareness?	Excellent	Fair	Below Average
Knowledge of colors that flatter you?	Excellent	Fair	Below Average
Knowledge of styles that flatter you?	Excellent	Fair	Below Average
Your image at work, play and home?	Excellent	Fair	Below Average

Which of the following terms best describe you (rank in order)….

_____ Classic_____ Dramatic_____ Elegant_____ Natural_____ Sporty

_____Other:

CREATIVE FASHION PROFILE (use back of page if needed)

1. What is the biggest fashion **mistake** you ever made?

2. What was your **best** fashion moment?

3. How would someone **describe** you in terms of your clothes?

4. What is the best **fashion advice** you have ever received?

5. Do you have a **signature piece** you wear all of the time?

6. What would you **never** be caught dead wearing?

7. If you had unlimited store credit, **where** would you shop?

8. Do you consider **shopping** to be a chore or a delight?

9.   Do you buy clothes based on **impulse** or do you plan your purchases?

10.   What do you **wish** you could wear but can't?

11.   What was your most **extravagant** fashion purchase?

12.   What fashion **magazines** do you read?

13.   What would you **change** about your current style?

14.   What's the one thing about **yourself** you'd like to change?

Write more:

NON-VERBAL COMMUNICATION STYLE

The following non-verbal communication points provide you an opportunity to effect change in your client and steer her toward success in life. Rate the client and make comments about your observations based on the subtle (and not so subtle) messages she is sending regarding her image and appearance. Be objective but not critical when you review these points with the client.

BODY LANGUAGE
Stance (i.e.: confident, shy, etc):

Posture (excellent, needs work, poor, etc):

Greeting style (reserved, emotional, friendly, etc):

Eye contact (shape of eyes, low/medium/high contact):

Handshake (loose, too soft, firm, too firm):

Voice (tone, quality, and pitch):

Language (accent, inflection, ability for small talk):

Eye movement when in conversation:

Body language (reflexive/non-reflexive/natural or forced)?

IMAGE REVIEW

Poise:

Manners:

Fashion style (defined, distinct, individual, confident, etc):

Communication component of dress (frazzled, clean, messy, etc):

Messages of appearance (economic, social, cultural):

Energy level (mellow, depressed, hyper, etc):

Choice of color in clothing:

Mannerisms or ticks:

Body odor:

Emotional expressions:

Facial expressions:

Other observations:

IMAGE REVIEW—CONTINUED

Quality of accessories:

Labels or brands represented:

Grooming:

Makeup:

Body modifications (tattoos, piercings, etc):

Smile quality:

Self-esteem:

Body confidence:

Other observations:

Did you notice areas that need adjustment or change? If so, then work with your client helping her make the appropriate changes to her image immediately. After all, the messages she is sending have an impact on how others treat her.

Enter your comments and observations here:

STEP 2 PHOTOGRAPH

Take before and after digital shots. Always take a headshot and a full body shot of before and after and keep as a record of the work you have done with the client.

Before and After Photos

Find a white wall in your studio. Using a digital camera take a close up shot of the client's face. Be sure her hair is pulled off the face (for accurate analysis later of her facial shape) and that she isn't wearing any makeup. Take a full body shot, without hands in pockets.

Hint: if you want a true "before" picture don't coach her first. Photograph her candid, as she is. See example above. Usually photos like this make for dramatic before and after results. Once you have the candid shot then:

- Have client take of eyeglasses.
- Have client relax and stand against white wall.
- Stand 8 feet away from her and sit on the floor to take a photo from a low angle.
- Take several photos, both front and side shots.

- Stand up for the close up of her neck and face. Take several shots. If she wears glasses take a shot with her wearing them and then a shot with glasses off.
- Remember you will be editing the background of these photos later so definitely stick with a white background for your photo.

When the client leaves and before your next session with her, edit the photos and file.

Notes:

STEP 3 MEASURE

BODY PROPORTION ANALYSIS

Date:_____ Client:_____

HORIZONTAL PLANE* BODY MEASUREMENTS:

1_____BUST   place measuring tape around chest at fullest part of bust line.

2_____WAIST   measure at the smallest part of the clients waist (do not worry about where the navel is).

3_____HIPS   measure the largest part of the derriere all the way around the body.

> Follow instructions on next page for vertical plane measurements:

4_____TOP OF HEAD TO FLOOR

5_____BUST TO FLOOR

6_____HIPS TO FLOOR

7_____MID-KNEE TO FLOOR

*A plane is used to describe the body's position when standing. Horizontal plane describes lines of the body that are parallel to the ground. A vertical plane describes lines of the body that run from foot to head and are used to describe if a body is balanced or not.

STEPS FOR MEASURING VERTICAL PLANE BODY SHAPE:

1) Tack printer paper on wall 7' up (you will make your marks on this paper, not on the wall!).

2) Have client take off shoes and stand facing you (back to the wall).

3) Take the ruler and rest on their head so it touches the wall.

4) Mark a pencil (or pen) mark on the paper where the ruler meets the wall (should be at the top of their head).

This is their height_____

5) Now mark where their bust (or chest) line meets the wall.

This is their bust to floor measurement_____

6) Now mark where their hips meet the wall.

This is their hip to floor measurement_____

7) Now mark where their knees meet the wall.

This is their knee to floor measurement_____

8) Record the results of 4-7 on the previous page (top of head, bust, hips, mid-knee).

This will determine their body balance - if they have a short torso, long waist, short legs or long legs and will help determine how to correct/ or camouflage any figure issues.

STEP 4 ANALYZE HORIZONTAL PLANE BODY SHAPE

Once you have your client's measurements you can use the following guidelines to determine her body shape. While the point is to enhance the shape the client has, the final goal is to achieve the illusion of an hourglass body shape, which is considered the fashion ideal. Use a ruler and work along one line only of the measurements.

For instance: this client measures 40" bust, 35" waist and 40" hips:

Line up a ruler at the 40" bust. If her waist and hip measurements line up in a straight line then you have found her bodyshape. We can see from the example below that she is NOT an inverted triangle. Go to the next bodyshape and line up the ruler - did you get the correct answer? Refer to the body shape charts at back of book to discover which of the 5 body shapes your client is.

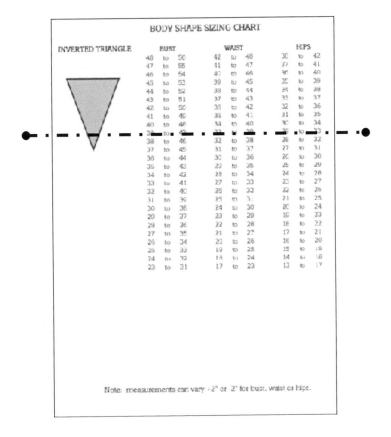

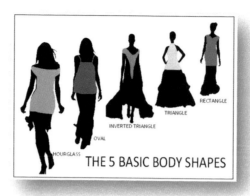

THE 5 BASIC BODY SHAPES

The five body shapes are detailed in the following pages. Note the before and after images for each body shape.

A balanced body shape is the most common of the vertical shapes. This is the easiest body shape to clothe because there is no need to camouflage or trick the viewer into seeing a balance. With short waisted and long waisted shapes the goal becomes to create a balanced body shape. Use clothing silhouettes and lines to either raise the waist (for long waisted) or lower the waist (short waisted).

HOURGLASS BODY SHAPE

◆ Waist that is 9" to 13" smaller than the bust and hip measurements
◆ Medium to large bust
◆ Waistline is narrower than bust line
◆ Hips area as wide as bust line
◆ Horizontal figure type versus vertical type (balanced)
◆ Has waist definition
◆ Has a proportioned body
◆ Legs are in proportion but this body type may also have shorter legs
◆ Facial shape also rounded – either oval, long oval or round

An hourglass figure is the ideal body shape. If client has this shape she can wear many silhouettes and does not need to rely on clothing camouflage tricks to create a flattering figure. Choose clothes to wear close to the body. Baggy and shapeless styles do nothing to flatter this look.

If her body is proportioned then she can wear lower cut waistlines on pants and has more room to play with clothing proportions. If not proportioned i.e.: torso is long or legs short, she will need to watch where to create the waistline in the clothes she wears.

Hourglass shapes by nature are curved and curved body shapes will have curved lines that extend over the body. The facial shape will also be curved. One typically sees oval, long oval, and round shaped faces with hourglass bodies.

ROUND BODY SHAPE (also diamond, oval)

- Apple shape, fullness at midriff
- Smaller shoulders and full neck
- Shape created by weight gain
- No waist definition
- Bust, waist and hips very close in measurements
- Horizontal body line
- Legs are in great shape
- May have short legs combined with broad shoulders
- Facial shape also curved and rounded

Proportion the top half of the body by wearing shoulder pads. Choose "V" necklines and vertical design lines (draped scarves, long necklaces, etc). Floral prints work well as long as they are medium in scale, not tiny and not oversized).

Create waist definition with visual accents such as seams, darts and lines. Dark solid colors on the inside, lighter colors on the outside (like a two piece suit with blouse underneath) work best as alternate outfits.

Wear skirts only if they fall past the knee and with the same color hose and shoes. Wear bold accessories above the bust-line (pins, chokers, etc.). Avoid wide waistbands, cropped pants and oversized dresses (especially caftans or muumuus).

TRIANGLE BODY SHAPE

- ◆ Small to medium size frame
- ◆ Narrow or sloping shoulders
- ◆ Hips wider that shoulders and bust line
- ◆ Body larger below the waist than above
- ◆ May have small bust line
- ◆ Large hips/ derriere
- ◆ Full legs, sometimes short legged
- ◆ Facial shapes usually with angles (square, triangle, diamond)

Balance the upper body by creating visual width - use shoulder pads and lighter colors on top, darker on the bottom. Wear tops with pleats, epaulets, ruffles, patch pockets. Wear simple and straight or slightly tapered pants without pleats or gathers at the waist.

Draw the eye upward with colorful accessories worn around the neckline and shoulder area. Avoid adding visual emphasis to the hip area with long jackets. Choose jackets that are cropped or box style.

INVERTED TRIANGLE BODY SHAPE

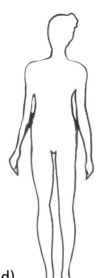

- ◆ Shoulders wider than the hips
- ◆ Body larger above the waist than below
- ◆ Small hips and flat derriere
- ◆ Great legs
- ◆ May have full bust
- ◆ Clothes hanger shoulders
- ◆ May have short legs combined with broad shoulders
- ◆ Sporty/ athletic physique
- ◆ Facial shapes usually with angles (square, triangle, diamond)

Wear darker colors on top, lighter colors on the bottom. "V" necks elongate the upper body. If wearing loose clothing that falls from the shoulders, belt at the waist to define a waistline. Gathered skirts and flared hems look great on this body type.

Wear wide legged trousers to create visual balance below the waist. Use horizontal stripes and patterns. This shape can wear halter tops well. Use accessories and jewelry to visually elongate the torso (scarves, long necklaces, etc.). Define the waist with belts or wrapped sashes.

RECTANGLE BODY SHAPE

Very little or no waist definition

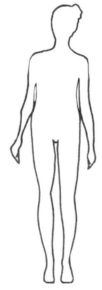

- Hips and shoulders look balanced
- Vertical body type (versus horizontal shape of an hourglass)
- Small derriere
- Legs are usually long
- Waist measures 1" to 8" smaller than bust
- Very common figure type as women age or gain weight
- This body type also known as "square"
- Facial shapes have sharp and square lines (square, triangle, diamond, heart)

Camouflage goal is to create an hourglass shape; a small waistline. Sure way to do this is to increase the shoulder width at the same time adding width to the hips. This will create the illusion of a small waist.

Wear fitted jackets with defined shoulders (pads, lines, seams, etc.). Wear wrap dresses with waist accents to help create the illusion of a waistline. Wear gathers and pleats at the waist.

Pants should be fitted with a slight flair at the bottom. Jackets with waist defining lines are good. Vertical lines will help elongate the figure. Depending on facial shape, wide necklines are also good.

DETERMINING VERTICAL PLANE BODY SHAPE

Horizontal body shape differs from vertical in that it is a determination of the body circumference. Vertical body shape (hourglass, round, rectangle, inverted triangle, triangle) is measured across the planes of the body and is the space relationship between shoulder to bust, bust to waist, waist to hips. Measuring a client for vertical body shape determines whether she is short waisted, long waisted, short legged, long legged or balanced.

Take a look at these illustrations. Note the line indicating the ideal waist for balanced body shape. For short waisted/ long legged body shape the waist line rises. Note, too, where the waist line drops on a figure indicating a long waist/ short legs.

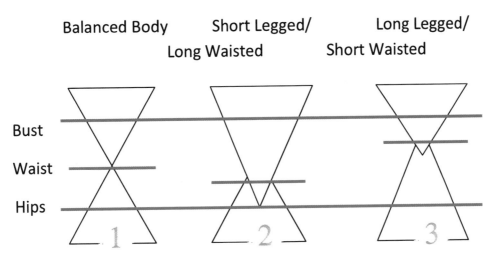

1. If the client's measurements between bust, waist and hip are the same she is balanced.
2. If her measurements between bust and waist are greater than between waist and hips then she is long waisted.
3. If her measurements are greater between waist and hips than between bust and waist she is short waisted.

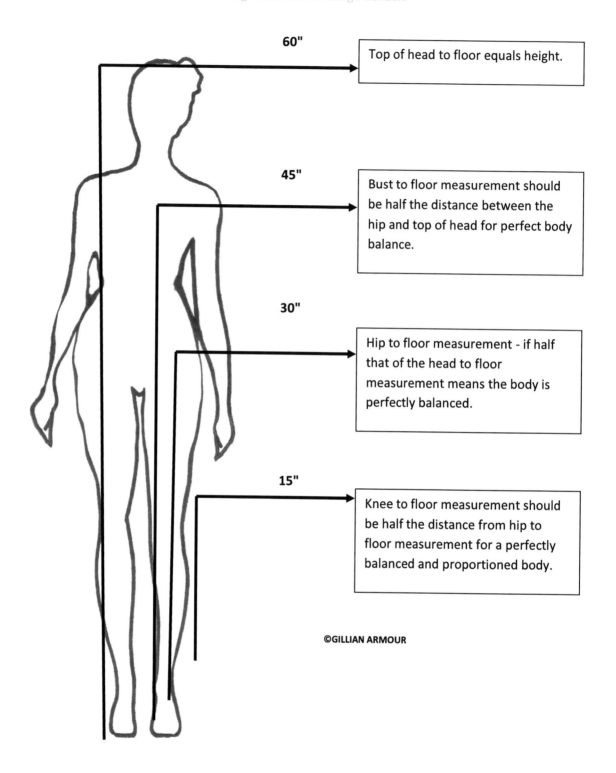

60"

Top of head to floor equals height.

45"

Bust to floor measurement should be half the distance between the hip and top of head for perfect body balance.

30"

Hip to floor measurement - if half that of the head to floor measurement means the body is perfectly balanced.

15"

Knee to floor measurement should be half the distance from hip to floor measurement for a perfectly balanced and proportioned body.

©GILLIAN ARMOUR

REVIEW FASHION RULES WITH THE CLIENT

The following fashion rules for shape shifting are universal for all figure types:

- Black *minimizes* any figure shape.
- White *maximizes* figure shape.
- Small prints emphasize large shapes.
- Large prints emphasize small shapes.
- One color head to toe creates length.
- One color on top and contrast on bottom cuts a shape in half; it appears shorter.
- Too tight or too loose is always too wrong.
- Age inappropriate dressing emphasizes your age.

This is a good time in the consultation to review the *Clothing Guide for Body Shapes* (sold separately) with the client. It's also a great time to discuss her personal style confusions, problems, and challenges. Since she now knows her body shape it should be easy for you to illustrate (through photos, magazine clippings, etc.) appropriate styles and silhouettes.

Of course you will need to know how to camouflage any figure flaws your client has by using shape shifting silhouettes of clothing. We have discussed a few of them here (the five body shapes above) to give you an idea of how to do this.

The general rule when image consulting on body shape is to create the illusion of an hourglass shape for women regardless of their existing body shape. If your client happens to be an hourglass then the work is easier for you! Remember, the hourglass shape is the fashion ideal and has been for thousands of years. It is the only shape of all the female figure shapes that has the most pleasing visual harmony for the viewers eye.

To give you an idea of how to dress appropriately we've gathered a few of our favorite examples of well dressed men and women before and after their fashion makeovers.

Before and After

Good on the left and better on the right. "Before" she styled her clothing silhouettes inappropriately for her body shape. The boxy jacket made her look boxier and the duo-tone colors of her clothes created a horizontal line that visually chopped her in half!

Before and After

Sloppy fit and incorrect silhouette gave this gentleman a frumpy look (on left). With a fitted suit and pants that suit his body frame he looks much better.

Before and After

Age and style appropriate. When clothing fits too tightly on the body, the image sends many messages, amongst them — I don't care, I have let myself go, I don't respect you enough to dress well for you and I have bad taste. These messages may or may not be true for the wearer, but for the viewer they are.

Before and After

When you know your body shape and size you know how to clothe and camouflage it. The goal is always to flatter a woman's body with clothing and not to insult it as we see here (on left).

Before and After

Business casual takes victims in the business environment. This young man might be the CEO of a technology firm but you'd never know it when he wears his jeans and t-shirts to work. With a suit and tie he gets the respect due him.

Before and After

Plus-size figures can look great in clothes that are proportioned and that flatter. The goal is to camouflage problem areas and to wear clothing lines that slim and lengthen. Here the client chooses colors that minimize and heighten (on right).

Before and After

Be careful how you represent yourself to the world. If you are trying to convey a feeling of youth because you have reached a certain age, do it appropriately – with flattering clothes and gorgeous accessories.

STEP 5 FACIAL SHAPE

By looking at your client, in person or photograph, determine facial shape using the criteria below. Later in this guide you will choose hairstyles for her facial shape. Use these guidelines when determining client facial shape. Knowing facial shape allows the client to choose (and you to recommend) appropriate eye glass styles, hairstyles, jewelry and makeup tips.

OVAL FACIAL SHAPE - This facial shape is egg shaped. It can also be a long oval; think of a long oval as an elongated egg shape. This face shape is equal in size across the face horizontally and down the face vertically and as such is perfectly proportioned. If you have this type of facial shape you can wear many styles, shapes and sizes of earrings, necklaces, scarves and hats.

HEART SHAPE is wider at the temples and tapers to a smaller almost pointy chin. Across the face from ear to ear is one width and from hairline to chin length is longer. Faces in this shape can be proportionally balanced by wearing jewelry styles that elogate the face. Earrings can be long drops in angular shapes for maximum flatter!

DIAMOND FACIAL SHAPE - Women with this facial shape have wide jawlines that stretch out to their ears. Typically they have wonderful cheekbones. To proportion this facial shape with jewelry seek to balance out the width by increasing visual length. Long drop shaped earrings will flatter a diamond shape, as will long necklaces and scarves tied below the collar bone.

SQUARE FACIAL SHAPE - Face shape is angular and equally as wide at the forehead, jawline and cheekbones. To proportion the face with jewelry choose earring styles that draw attention vertically across the cheeks and continuing down the neck. Large chandelier shaped earrings work well for this purpose.

ROUND FACIAL SHAPE - This particular shape is wide throughout the jaw and cheek area, almost a filled out oval shape and can wear many styles of earring and necklace as long as the proportion of visual interest is vertical (to elongate the face) and not horizontal (which will widen the face).

TRIANGLE FACIAL SHAPE - has a wider jawline and narrower temple. The best jewels are ones that, when worn, will widen the face at the cheekbone. Earrings that are dramatic, bold, and big, worn close to the ear, are the most flattering for this facial shape. The best neckwear can include long necklaces to elongate the neck. Chokers and wrapped scarves do not flatter this facial shape.

Sketch your client's facial shape here and compare with the above shapes:

STEP 6 HAIRSTYLES

Flattering hairstyles happen when they match the facial shape of the wearer. Make sure you know your client's face shape before you suggest hairstyles. A great way to confirm her face shape and to choose flattering styles for her is to visit an on-line site that specializes in hairstyles by facial shape. One of my favorites is www.myshape.com but there are others. I recommend you do some research online and find the site that is the most user friendly for you and your client.

Here are the tried and true rules to determining face shape:

Using a soft measuring tape:

1. Measure client's face across the top of the cheekbones. Write down the measurement on a piece of paper.

2. Measure across her jaw line from the widest point to the widest point. Write down the measurement.

3. Measure across her forehead at the widest point. Generally the widest point will be halfway between eyebrows and hairline. Write down the measurement.

4. Measure from the tip of hairline to the bottom of chin.

The following internet sites provide you the tools to determine facial shape. Using a digital image of your client, you can upload it to a site, and within a matter of minutes have hairstyle, jewelry, and eyeglass examples that flatter her particular facial shape.

www.dailymakeover.com
www.thehairstyler.com
www.visualmakeover.com

QUICK METHOD FOR FACIAL SHAPE DETERMINATION

MEASURE ACROSS FOREHEAD

MEASURE TIP OF HAIRLINE TO BOTTOM OF CHIN

MEASURE ACROSS CHEEKBONE

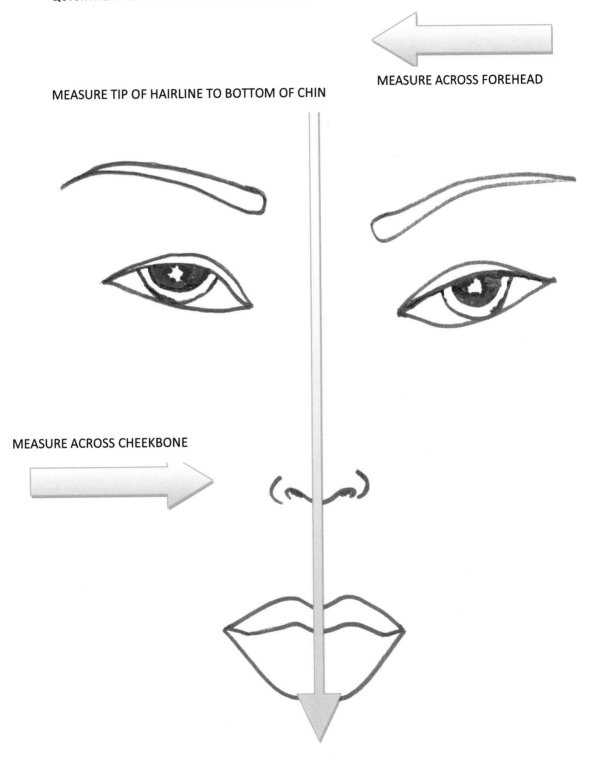

- *Oval*: This type of face is very oval-shaped and equal in size on top and bottom.

- *Heart*: Wider at the temples and narrower at the chin.

- *Round*: This face type is similar to the oval, but shorter.

- *Triangle*: The opposite of the heart, this type of face is usually wide at the chin with a narrow forehead.

- *Square*: A strong jaw and squared-off features are typical of this type.

- *Rectangle*: A longer version of the square face.

- *Diamond*: Widest at cheekbones, narrow forehead and jaw line of approximately equal widths.

Go Long to Slim the Face

For round faces, the worst thing you can do is to get a chin length cut. That will just draw attention to the roundness of the face. To make your face look longer and slimmer, keep hair long, at least shoulder length. While some layering at the bottom can work, it is usually best to keep layers out of the face and below the jaw line. Longer styles also go very well with an oval-shaped face.

Use Bangs to Hide Flaws

Bangs camouflage a large forehead or are often used to soften a face. Bangs usually look best when they are not too full, so stick to just a light coverage. Bangs go well with heart-shaped faces to minimize the width of the forehead, and are also ideal for softening a square or rectangular face. Avoid using them with a round face shape, since this will cut off length and make the face look even shorter.

Layers Create Softness

When you have straight lines in your face, such as those with a square or rectangular face, some well-placed layers can really help soften your face and create a more feminine look. Be careful of having too many layers, since this can actually start to look frizzy and unkempt, but a handful of wisps looks great.

Short Hairstyles Add Width to the Jaw

Obviously, if you already have a naturally wide chin, you won't want to opt for a bob or any other chin-length cut. However, for heart-shaped faces, this is the ideal hairstyle to balance out the wide forehead. Short hair can also be used successfully with a rectangular face, to create a shorter look, particularly if combined with a layered cut to add texture and softness to the face.

Add Some Curl For Extra Body

Not everyone is blessed with full hair and when you have a triangular or a rectangular face, a little extra volume can really help. Going with a light perm or curl can help add some volume to your hair and balance out these face types. Now that you have a fairly good idea of what your face shape is and which hairstyles compliment it, you can take a look at a variety of hairstyles from magazines, the Internet or hairstylists' style books and decide which is the right one for your face. Choosing the best hairstyle for you will result in a great look that enhances your natural beauty and makes you feel your best everyday.

STEP 7 STYLE PERSONALITY

Part of being a successful image consultant is knowing how to bring your client's personal style to the fore. To bring out her style we've developed a very successful and easy method called the Style Personality Quiz.

Use the following modified STYLE PERSONALITY QUIZ and work through each question with your client. This gives you and she an opportunity to discuss her present image and to develop a new one. When you have discovered her clothing style personality, offer her examples of how this personality is translated into the clothing and accessories she will wear (dramatic personalities do well to add big bold splashes of colorful accessories, whereas romantic personalities incorporate antique jewels into their looks).

Client Book Sold Separately

Circle each letter that seems the truest statement of your client's current style. There are no right or wrong answers to these statements. As an image consultant it's your job to uncover a style personality for your client. You can use adjectives to sum up her personality based on what you discover or refer to the descriptions following this quiz. Facilitate the quiz with her:

1) I define my clothing choices as:

   a) Comfort first, always
   b) I can't stand clutter. Everything must have a purpose
   c) My clothes have to be pretty – for casual, work or dressy occasions
   d) Aside from a few, around-the-house items, all my clothes make a statement
   e) The wackier, more diverse, more impossible the better
   f) Order and simplicity. Everything must be up-to-date and mix and match

2) I prefer work clothes that are:

   a) Separates that mix and match, comfortable yet smart
   b) Classically tailored clothes
   c) Preferably softer, fluid designs
   d) Bold combinations
   e) Individual but appropriate
   f) Elegantly blended neutral colors

3) For weekends I prefer:

   a) Casual, relaxed gear
   b) A timeless, good quality skirt and sweater
   c) Pretty blouses and tops; nice shoes
   d) Something WOW
   e) Ethnic, avant-garde, unpredictable styling
   f) Simple but so chic

4) My best hairstyle is:

   a) Casual and windblown, natural
   b) Controlled and neat but not severe
   c) A soft, layered look, never short
   d) Something modern; my style changes all the time
   e) Spiky, loose curls; I use scarves and clips a lot
   f) Current, but timeless, in great condition

5) Fabrics I love include:

   a) Denim, knits, anything textured
   b) Natural fabrics; 100% wool, cotton, silk, organic
   c) Jersey, soft, lace, silk and vintage
   d) Rich velvets, brocades, suede's and corduroy
   e) Metallic's, leather, contrasting textures like tweed
   f) Best quality wool crepe, cashmere, linen, dupionis

6) The accessories I prefer:

   a) Not much, preferably natural beads and stones
   b) Pearls and gold
   c) Delicate chains and antique jewels
   d) Striking, bold pieces, one of a kind
   e) Ethnic, I like to layer them on
   f) Real jewels and quality costume, designer pieces

7) For evening I like to wear:

   a) A nice pantsuit
   b) Simple black dress, knee length
   c) A gorgeous dress with lots of detailing, vintage
   d) Colorful silk kimono or tunic with a skirt or pants
   e) Full length kimono with all the accessories
   f) Smoking jacket and matching trousers

8) My shoes are usually:

   a) Sneakers, high tops or walking shoes
   b) Flats or very low heels
   c) Higher heels with embellishments
   d) Smart boots or what's currently in style
   e) Funky styles, ballet flats to platforms
   f) A slight heel in a classic shape

9) My favorite colors are:

   a) Naturals, nothing bright or neon
   b) Blended colors but no bold colors
   c) Feminine pastels
   d) Rich and bold colors with black and white
   e) Neon, hand painted, brights
   f) Neutral colors, charcoal, pewter, ivory and cream

10) My style icons are:

   a) Katherine Hepburn, Marcia Cross, Diane Keaton
   b) Angelina Jolie, Victoria Beckham, Ivanka Trump
   c) Heidi Klum, Katie Holmes, Mary Kate Olson
   d) Cher, Rihanna, Janice Dickinson
   e) Tilda Swinton, Bjork, Madonna
   f) Michelle Obama, Brooke Shields, Nicole Kidman

11) When I shop I:

   a) Spend as little time as possible shopping
   b) I only buy when I need something new
   c) I buy clothes that I think others will like
   d) I buy the latest and greatest
   e) I am always looking for something no one else has
   f) I buy the best quality I can afford

Place a check mark in each box for each answer:

Question	A	B	C	D	E	F
1						
2						
3						
4						
5						
6						
7						
8						
9						
10						
11						
TOTAL						

- Enter and add the total amount of your answers in each column into the bottom row marked TOTAL.
- The column with the highest number of answers reveals your STYLE PERSONALITY – see below.

A. Conservative, Smart, Practical
B. Classic, Modern, Poised
C. Romantic, Vintage, Charming
D. Dramatic, Independent, Sexy
E. Artistic, Creative, Passionate
F. Elegant, Cultured, Classy

Notes:

STYLE PERSONALITIES

Conservative, Smart, Practical

You love high quality fabrics such as tweeds, cashmeres and crisp pure cotton. Your look is Ivy League with a personal touch. You love wearing crisp white blouses paired with gray wool slacks and will add antique rhinestone and pearl jewels as a style stamp. You don't spend frivolously and your wardrobe is filled with conservative styles that will last the test of time. Your taste and choice in clothing mirrors most European women's.

Classic, Modern, Poised

You also love quality fabrics but your clothing choices lean toward classic and elegant. Your color choices are always modern. For instance, you will buy a cashmere jacket in a gorgeous pink color. You look and feel great in Garbo pants with a tailored navy sailor jacket.

Romantic, Vintage, Charming

Soft ruffles, lace, antique buttons: these are details you pay close attention to when choosing your clothing. You love to shop vintage clothing stores and have a stash of vintage slips you love to wear. Modern styles have to have romantic elements. You love hand-made and your jewelry matches this mood.

Dramatic, Independent, Sexy

Your clothing choices are always bold, confident and body conscious. You are not afraid to mix colors, patterns and styles from today's designers. You are in love with black lace and corsetry.

Artistic, Creative, Passionate

You, more than any other clothing personality, have an intense interest in color, texture, pattern and print and have the confidence to combine these elements in your dress and accessories. You always have the best shoes and bags.

Elegant, Cultured, Classy

You are a couture fan and enjoy hand tailored clothing. Pearls and heirloom gold add dash to your cashmere jackets and silk trousers. You love wearing simple and elegant styles. If you could you would wear 1930's fashion all the time.

STEP 8 FASHION STYLE/ SCRAPBOOKING

Now that you have a clear idea of your client's personal likes and dislikes, body shape and style personality you have all the ammo you need to create a style story. Follow these steps to illustrate for the client the types of clothing she should be wearing and how these clothes convey the most appropriate image for her.

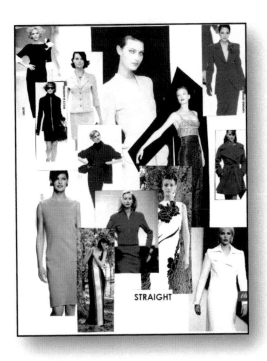

My clients love this project. It bonds us and teaches at the same time.

- Set up a table with blank sheets of paper, scissors, glue and a handful of recent fashion magazines.
- Have your client go through the magazines to pull out photos of clothing she thinks are suited to her bodyshape and personality. Guide her along by editing her choices. She may start out choosing incorrect clothing silhouettes or fashion styles.
- When your client has several examples pulled, collage them onto the paper. Discuss the relevance of each outfit to her bodyshape (does it flatter, is it congruent with her personality, etc.).
- Encourage her to add inspiring images that speak about her personality.

She then takes this collage with her and can add to it at home. Explain that these storyboards need to be updated regularly and encourage her to make another appointment with you in about three months. Be sure to scan the collage and add it to her files for future reference.

COLLAGE

SAMPLES OF BODY SHAPE COLLAGES

CURVED

SOFT

SHARP STRAIGHT

SOFT STRAIGHT

SOFT CURVED

STRAIGHT

STEP 9 MAKEUP

This is an optional service for clients. It's a great add on and an easy sell if your client wants your expertise. Optionally, she can use this form for a visit to the makeup counter and a makeup consult at her favorite makeup line.

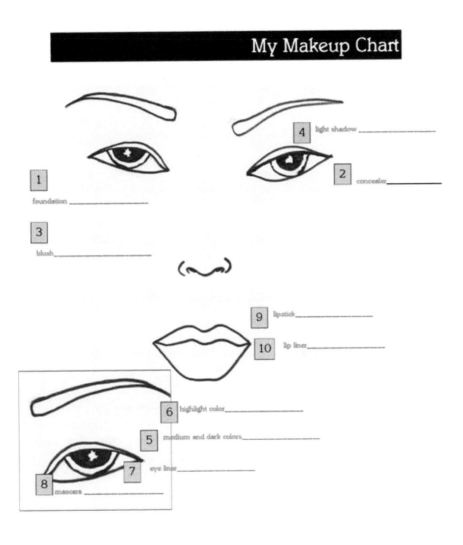

Creating Makeup Charts – work through this with your clients. Use the facial diagram included in the forms section to color in (you will need makeup and brushes to color directly onto the paper). You can also do a separate makeup application session with your client using makup samples.

STEP 10 WARDROBE

Use these forms to facilitate a closet or wardrobe session with clients. Review their clothing needs; list and use this as a shopping list. This is another option for your client to book your services.

Take digital photos of coordinated outfits as you go through her closet. Send her this digital file later for easy reference to coordinating clothing from her closet.

STEP 1 CLOSET INVENTORY - make a list of
items in client's closet and decide to keep, fix, tailor or donate.

STEP 2 WARDROBE PLANNER - use this worksheet to create coordinated
outfits from the edited clothing pile.

STEP 3 FOUNDATION PLAN - for a nine piece coordinated set of clothing.
With just 9 pieces from her wardrobe that match these silhouettes she can create 42 separate and matched outfits.

STEP 4 OUTFIT PLANNER - gives you the option of creating Business Casual,
Business Dressy, Business to Event or Event outfits.

STEP 5 ACCESSORY WORKSHEET - use this worksheet to coordinate
jewels, hats, purses, shoes, etc. with outfits.

FORMS & WORKSHEETS

Step 1

CLOSET INVENTORY

Client_____
Date_____

ITEM	DESCRIPTION	RATING	DECIDE	ACTION
PANT	Blue jean with red patches	4	Fix	fixed

Rating: 1 = I hate it, 2 = Not crazy about it, 3 = Like it, 4 = Love it & keeping it
Decide: Keep, Fix, Clean, Toss, Donate

Step 2

WARDROBE PLANNER WORKSHEET

CLIENT NAME:

Step 1 Write an inventory of all clothing items client is keeping AFTER closet edit (any damaged, unwanted or inappropriate clothing tossed)

Blouses	Jackets	Tops	Pants	Jeans	Skirts	Dresses	Long Jackets

Notes:

Step 3

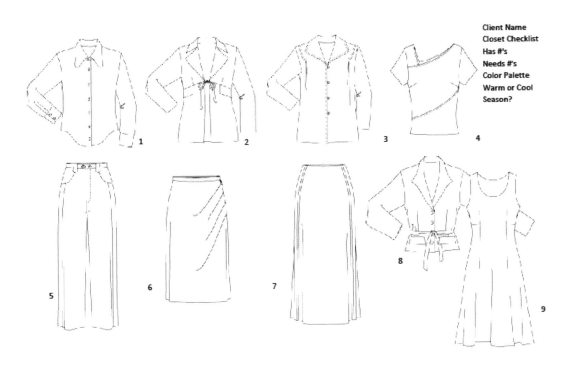

Client Name
Closet Checklist
Has #'s
Needs #'s
Color Palette
Warm or Cool
Season?

1) Blouse 2) Tie front jacket 3) Button front jacket does double duty as a blouse 4) Wrap top 5) Jean or plain pant
6) Skirt with detailing 7) Mid length skirt 8) Tie waist jacket 9) Sleeveless dress.
These 9 fashion basic pieces can be combined to create 42 separate outfits. Shown here are blanks. Just color in and go. For example - if your client
has these shapes in varying colors, prints and textures use copies of this sheet to help her organize outfits to wear.

This worksheet details the nine silhouettes you will need to in order to create up to 42 separate outfits. Choose two or three colors from your existing wardrobe or purchase nine items in coordinating colors. You will have many outfits as a result.

Step 4

PLAN AN OUTFIT

Client Name: Description:	OUTFIT 1 Business Casual	OUTFIT 2 Business Dressy	OUTFIT 3 Business to Event	OUTFIT 4 Event
1 Blouse				
2 Jacket				
3 Jacket				
4 Top				
5 Pant				
6 Jean				
7 Skirt				
8 Skirt				
9 Dress				

ACCESSORY WORKSHEET

Client_____
Date_____

ACCESSORY/JEWEL	WEAR WITH	WHEN
gold necklace	white shirt. Grey pants	office
Pink scarf	Cream silk blouse/ black pants	Early Cocktail party

BODY SHAPE MEASUREMENT CHARTS
HOURGLASS SHAPE

BUST				WAIST				HIPS		
48	TO	50		36	TO	40		48	TO	50
47	TO	49		35	TO	39		47	TO	49
46	TO	48		34	TO	38		46	TO	48
45	TO	47		33	TO	37		45	TO	47
44	TO	46		32	TO	36		44	TO	46
43	TO	45		31	TO	35		43	TO	45
42	TO	44		30	TO	34		42	TO	44
41	TO	43		29	TO	33		41	TO	43
40	TO	42		28	TO	32		40	TO	42
39	TO	41		27	TO	31		39	TO	41
38	TO	40		26	TO	30		38	TO	40
37	TO	39		25	TO	29		37	TO	39
36	TO	38		24	TO	28		36	TO	38
35	TO	37		23	TO	27		35	TO	37
34	TO	36		22	TO	26		34	TO	36
33	TO	35		21	TO	25		33	TO	35
32	TO	34		20	TO	24		32	TO	34
31	TO	33		19	TO	23		31	TO	33
30	TO	32		18	TO	22		30	TO	32
29	TO	31		17	TO	21		29	TO	31
28	TO	30		16	TO	20		28	TO	30
27	TO	29		15	TO	19		27	TO	29
26	TO	28		14	TO	18		26	TO	28
25	TO	27		13	TO	17		25	TO	27
24	TO	26		12	TO	16		24	TO	26

Hold ruler in a straight line across this chart. If clients measurements do not align straight across then move to the next chart and so on until you determine actual body shape.

ROUND, OVAL OR DIAMOND SHAPE

BUST			WAIST			HIPS		
48	TO	51	53	TO	56	48	TO	51
47	TO	50	52	TO	55	47	TO	50
46	TO	49	51	TO	54	46	TO	49
45	TO	48	50	TO	53	45	TO	48
44	TO	47	49	TO	52	44	TO	47
43	TO	46	48	TO	51	43	TO	46
42	TO	45	47	TO	50	42	TO	45
41	TO	44	46	TO	49	41	TO	44
40	TO	43	45	TO	48	40	TO	43
39	TO	42	44	TO	47	39	TO	42
38	TO	41	43	TO	46	38	TO	41
37	TO	40	42	TO	45	37	TO	40
36	TO	39	41	TO	44	36	TO	39
35	TO	38	40	TO	43	35	TO	38
34	TO	37	39	TO	42	34	TO	37
33	TO	36	38	TO	41	33	TO	36
32	TO	35	37	TO	40	32	TO	35
31	TO	34	36	TO	39	31	TO	34
30	TO	33	35	TO	38	30	TO	33
29	TO	32	34	TO	37	29	TO	32
28	TO	31	33	TO	36	28	TO	31
27	TO	30	32	TO	35	27	TO	30
26	TO	29	31	TO	34	26	TO	29
25	TO	28	30	TO	33	25	TO	28
24	TO	27	29	TO	32	24	TO	27

Hold ruler in a straight line across this chart. If clients measurements do not align straight across then move to the next chart and so on until you determine actual body shape.

TRIANGLE BODY SHAPE

BUST				WAIST				HIPS		
48	TO	51		43	TO	46		47	TO	57
47	TO	50		42	TO	45		46	TO	56
46	TO	49		41	TO	44		45	TO	55
45	TO	48		40	TO	43		44	TO	54
44	TO	47		39	TO	42		43	TO	53
43	TO	46		38	TO	41		42	TO	52
42	TO	45		37	TO	40		41	TO	51
41	TO	44		36	TO	39		40	TO	50
40	TO	43		35	TO	38		39	TO	49
39	TO	42		34	TO	37		38	TO	48
38	TO	41		33	TO	36		37	TO	47
37	TO	40		32	TO	35		36	TO	46
36	TO	39		31	TO	34		35	TO	45
35	TO	38		30	TO	33		34	TO	44
34	TO	37		29	TO	32		33	TO	43
33	TO	36		28	TO	31		32	TO	42
32	TO	35		27	TO	30		31	TO	41
31	TO	34		26	TO	29		30	TO	40
30	TO	33		25	TO	28		29	TO	39
29	TO	32		24	TO	27		28	TO	38
28	TO	31		23	TO	26		27	TO	37
27	TO	30		22	TO	25		26	TO	36
26	TO	29		21	TO	24		25	TO	35
25	TO	28		20	TO	23		24	TO	34
24	TO	27		19	TO	22		23	TO	33

Hold ruler in a straight line across this chart. If clients measurements do not align straight across then move to the next chart and so on until you determine actual body shape.

INVERTED TRIANGLE BODY SHAPE

BUST			WAIST			HIPS		
48	TO	51	43	TO	46	43	TO	46
47	TO	50	42	TO	45	42	TO	45
46	TO	49	41	TO	44	41	TO	44
45	TO	48	40	TO	43	40	TO	43
44	TO	47	39	TO	42	39	TO	42
43	TO	46	38	TO	41	38	TO	41
42	TO	45	37	TO	40	37	TO	40
41	TO	44	36	TO	39	36	TO	39
40	TO	43	35	TO	38	35	TO	38
39	TO	42	34	TO	37	34	TO	37
38	TO	41	33	TO	36	33	TO	36
37	TO	40	32	TO	35	32	TO	35
36	TO	39	31	TO	34	31	TO	34
35	TO	38	30	TO	33	30	TO	33
34	TO	37	29	TO	32	29	TO	32
33	TO	36	28	TO	31	28	TO	31
32	TO	35	27	TO	30	27	TO	30
31	TO	34	26	TO	29	26	TO	29
30	TO	33	25	TO	28	25	TO	28
29	TO	32	24	TO	27	24	TO	27
28	TO	31	23	TO	26	23	TO	26
27	TO	30	22	TO	25	22	TO	25
26	TO	29	21	TO	24	21	TO	24
25	TO	28	20	TO	23	20	TO	23
24	TO	27	19	TO	22	19	TO	22

Hold ruler in a straight line across this chart. If clients measurements do not align straight across then move to the next chart and so on until you determine actual body shape.

RECTANGLE BODY SHAPE

BUST				WAIST				HIPS		
48	TO	51		45	TO	48		47	TO	50
47	TO	50		44	TO	47		46	TO	49
46	TO	49		43	TO	46		45	TO	48
45	TO	48		42	TO	45		44	TO	47
44	TO	47		41	TO	44		43	TO	46
43	TO	46		40	TO	43		42	TO	45
42	TO	45		39	TO	42		41	TO	44
41	TO	44		38	TO	41		40	TO	43
40	TO	43		37	TO	40		39	TO	42
39	TO	42		36	TO	39		38	TO	41
38	TO	41		35	TO	38		37	TO	40
37	TO	40		34	TO	37		36	TO	39
36	TO	39		33	TO	36		35	TO	38
35	TO	38		32	TO	35		34	TO	37
34	TO	37		31	TO	34		33	TO	36
33	TO	36		30	TO	33		32	TO	35
32	TO	35		29	TO	32		31	TO	34
31	TO	34		28	TO	31		30	TO	33
30	TO	33		27	TO	30		29	TO	32
29	TO	32		26	TO	29		28	TO	31
28	TO	31		25	TO	28		27	TO	30
27	TO	30		24	TO	27		26	TO	29
26	TO	29		23	TO	26		25	TO	28
25	TO	28		22	TO	25		24	TO	27
24	TO	27		21	TO	24		23	TO	26

Hold ruler in a straight line across this chart. If clients measurements do not align straight across then move to the next chart and so on until you determine actual body shape.

MAKEUP MODULE

Makeup affords women a simple, effective and inexpensive way to dramatically enhance or change our appearance.

The right makeup color and application can make us positively glow, while the wrong makeup color or application can ruin an otherwise perfect look.

This guide will take you through the basic steps of makeup application, and then give you some guidelines for selecting your makeup colors and tools. At the back of this book you will find a face chart to use when testing makeup at the makeup counter.

YOUR FACE IN TEN STEPS

Makeup application done well can take years off your face and make you look and feel wonderful. This guide is simplified into 10 steps. Making up your face should take you about 5 to 10 minutes at the most. Simple, perfectly applied makeup can help you put together a polished working image. A stylish, balanced look will make you feel really confident and ready to face the day.

STEP ONE/ CONCEALER

Concealers are a fast and effective way to cover up lines, spots or shadows. Use them to hide scars, blotches or veins, not just to get perfect looking skin but to build a canvas on which to paint in the rest of your makeup.

Corrective concealers are a concentrated form of foundation and come is a range of colors. Find one that matches your skin tone.

Color concealers typically come in 3 color choices- **green**, yellow, and **lavender** (mauve). You need to understand which color concealer will neutralize the flaw. Look at the flaw you want to cover. What color is it? Is it acne (red) or under-eye circles (blue)? By identifying this first, you are now ready to conceal those nasty little imperfections! Here's a list of color concealers and what they neutralize:

Yellow concealer: Use to conceal bluish bruises, under-eye circles and mild red tones on the face.

Lavender concealer: Use to normalize yellow-colored skin imperfections such as sallow complexions and yellow bruises. It can also help conceal very dark under-eye circles and dark spots on bronze skin tones.

Green concealer: Use to neutralize red tones on the skin. Use green concealer for covering blemishes, pimples, red blotches, rosacea, port-wine stains.

STEP TWO/ FOUNDATION

Foundation is well named - it is the base upon which your face is painted. Once your foundation is applied your skin as canvas is ready to paint!

Foundation comes in a cream, liquid, or cake form. If you have oily skin use water based liquid and apply with a sponge. If your skin is normal with dry spots use an oil based foundation. Be careful to match your foundation (also known as base) to the skin along your jaw line. Apply a small dot of foundation, blend in to the skin and if you can't see the makeup after you have blended it in, then that's the right shade for you. Do this test under lighting and in front of a mirror. Test foundation on the inside of the forearm where the skin tone color is closest to the color on the neck near your face. Makeup should blend with the skin of the neck and jawbone.

Do's and Don'ts for applying foundation:

- Don't apply foundation to dirty or sweaty skin as this will clog pores and encourage pimples and acne.
- Don't apply foundation to your neck area as the skin here is thinner and not the same shade as your face. You will be two toned and, besides that, you run the risk of getting makeup on your clothing.
- Do apply just enough so that your concealer is concealed. Too much foundation and all your wrinkles will start to show.
- Don't apply foundation to skin that is breaking out. If you have to wear foundation choose a medicated or custom blended product that contains natural and mineral ingredients.

Do apply foundation in *up and out* strokes using a sponge applicator. Rinse these applicators between foundation applications but do not use soap as this will irritate your skin the next time you apply your base.

STEP THREE/ POWDER

Powder gives your face an evenness and, if applied properly, a healthy sheen. It also sets your foundation so it stays put and looks good longer. It is a final layer to concealing lines or skin blemishes that concealer and foundation aren't able to cover.

A translucent or colorless powder is the best. A mineral based powder even better.

Powders come in pressed or loose form. You will need to use a powder brush to apply either form.

Loose powder gives the best coverage and lasts longer. Dust it lightly over your entire face then shake off any excess powder and brush over your face one more time to blend.

Pressed powders come in compact form, sometimes with individual applicators. DO NOT use these applicators. They are usually cotton or synthetic fabric and will remove your concealer and base foundation. Always use a powder brush (large and soft) to apply powders.

Choose a skin tone match the same way you do with foundation - by applying a small amount of powder to your jaw line and watching how it disappears with your skin tone.

Apply powder in downward strokes and follow the way your facial hair grows to avoid lumps and clumps.

STEP FOUR/ BLUSH

Blush is applied to create a youthful, healthy look. Indeed, it is applied to the apples of the cheeks to give a fresh scrubbed "natural" glow to the skin.

Blush comes in powder or cake form and is always applied with a brush, never a sponge. Use blush sparingly as a little goes a long way.

Powder blush - this should be applied over your foundation. Dip your brush, tap off excess, and make a smile. Where the apples of your cheek lift is where you apply the blush. Move in an upward motion toward your outer eye. Blend a few times making sure that the color looks natural.

Cream blusher - applying cream blusher breaks the rules of makeup and is one of only a few times when you will use your fingers to apply color.

Start with a small dab of blush and apply to the apple of your cheek.

Blend, blend, and blend to get a soft glow. Again, you do not want to see the blush sitting on your face. It must blend in.

You can also use a foundation sponge wedge instead of fingers.

COLOR CHOICES:

To gauge your best makeup colors you'll need to take a look at the underlying skin shade of your face. If you haven't already had your colors analyzed, the easiest way to discover if you are a cool based or warm based undertone is to test at the makeup counter. Makeup artists can diagnose you swiftly.

YOUR COLORING	YOUR MAKEUP FAMILY
Dark Hair/ Olive Skin	Warm Brown
Red Hair/ Warm Skin	Warm Peach
Red Hair/ Cool Skin	Soft Peach
Dark Hair/ Warm Skin	Rosy Brown
Dark Hair/ Cool Skin	Cool Rose
Blonde Hair/ Warm Skin	Tawny Pink
Blond Hair/ Cool Skin	Baby Pink

STEP 5/ EYEBROWS

Eyebrows are the frames of the eyes and need your attention. Usually neglected, over plucked and sometimes shaved, the eyebrow has the power to make your face come alive with personality. Take a lesson is plucking, or get them professionally shaped.

To define your eyebrows use a pencil or powder applied with an eyebrow brush. Have your eyebrow comb ready to finish with gel. The gel will set the eyebrows in place. Ideally you should use a slanted (angled) brush for eyebrows.

Start by combing the eyebrow hairs down. Find the top of the eyebrow arch. Dip your angled brush into powder and starting at the arch draw a line of powder across the top of the eyebrow down toward the outer eye. Dip the brush a second time and make another line (or two) from the beginning of your eyebrow nearer to the nose and draw in to meet the arch line.

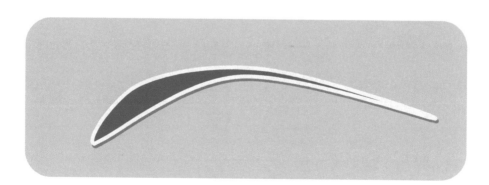

STEP 6/ EYESHADOW

Eye shadow comes in powder, stick, liquid and cream form. You can also have it applied via airbrush!

Powder eye shadows are the most popular and come in pressed powder containers usually with an applicator. Do not use the applicator. Instead use one of your brushes.

Using a damp sponge head applicator for powders will make them darker - perfect for evening looks.

- Start with a neutral ivory powder on your sponge applicator.
- Sweep it over your lid and out toward the outer eye. This is your base eye makeup.
- Using another, smaller sponge head applicator, apply a medium dark color into the fold of your eye lid.
- Then take a larger brush and apply a highlight color to the brow bone under your eyebrow.
- Use a liquid liner for the lid and then sweep a final brush of neutral powder over your lid.

STEP 7/ EYELINER

Eyeliner also comes in liquid, powder or pencil form. You can even find it in felt-tip pen! You can use several types on your upper lids.

For your lower lids (under your lower eyelashes) it's best to use cream pencil for easy smudging.

You can apply eyeliner either with sharp edges or with soft and smoky edges.

- Looking down into a mirror and keeping your hand steady, apply liquid eyeliner along your upper lashes.
- Use a clean cotton swab to work some brown eye shadow under your lower lashes to add some subtle definition.
- The perfect eyeliner is one that matches the color in the outer ring of the iris in your eye.
- Eyeliner defines the eyes and can make them look smaller. If your eyes are already on the small side just apply liner to the upper lashes and not the lower.
- Close set eyes do better when the lines are smudged and applied from the center of the lasher out toward the eye corner.

STEP 8/ MASCARA

Mascara is an invaluable way to create a flattering frame for the eyes. Most mascara come in a wand-like applicator and are easy to apply to the lashes. There are many varieties of lash thickening mascara on the market these days, many in colors like blue, green, gold and even red! This favorite tool of women can be found in most makeup bags.

Start by applying mascara to your upper lashes. Brush the tops down to the tips and then brush from the bottom of the lash to the tips. Repeat this step for your bottom lashes. To fill in any missing lashes take the wand and with zigzag motions move it over the top lashes and then the lower lashes.

Wait a few seconds for the mascara to dry and then blink. If any clumps appear use a Q-tip™ cotton swab and gently smooth out the lashes.

STEP 9/ LIP LINER

Lip liners are used to provide an outline for your lips prior to applying lipstick or lip gloss. Liner should be applied to treated lips. Use a clear matte lip salve to prepare your lip. Apply the liner to the entire outer line of your lip. Lip liner can also be used to camouflage or correct miss-shaped or irregular shaped lips.

- Use the lip liner to draw the outer silhouette and your lipstick to fill in the color. It's important to match your lip liner as closely as possible with your lipstick.

- Applying lip liner to the entire lip area keeps lips colored even when your lipstick wears off.

- Outline your lips with a color slightly darker than your shade of lipstick.

- Use color to create the illusion of fuller lips by darkening the edges of the lips.

- To define downward sloping lips draw lip liner slightly higher on the upper lip.

STEP 10/ LIPSTICK

Lipstick is the easiest and fastest way to give your face a splash of color. Lipsticks come in bullet form, pot of color, gloss and brush on. Lipsticks in bullet form are the most popular way to use lip color. The more pigment in a lipstick the longer it will last on your lips. Use your lip brush to apply and carefully paint on color.

Gloss can also be applied using a brush. You can use gloss alone or to top off your lipstick.

- Prime your lips with clear matte lip salve (balm).

- Apply lip liner first – apply around the edges of the lips first, then color in the entire lip area. This keeps your lips colored even after lipstick wears off.

- Stroke your lip brush over the tip of the lipstick, pick up color and get ready to paint your lips.

- Draw your lips tight over your teeth in a forced smile.

- Fill in the outline you created with the lip liner with the lipstick color for a shiny finish.

- Dab with a Kleenex™ or top with lip gloss.

FACE PLAY - LIST YOUR PERSONAL COLORS HERE:

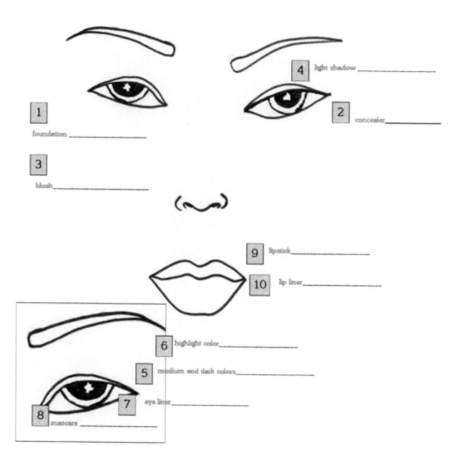

4 light shadow _____

1

2 concealer _____

foundation _____

3

blush _____

9 lipstick _____

10 lip liner _____

6 highlight color _____

5 medium and dark colors _____

7 eye liner _____

8 mascara _____

BRUSH UP YOUR MAKEUP

Successful make-up application depends on the tools you use. While it's fine to use your fingertips for some jobs it's always better to use proper tools. Here is a list of basic makeup tools you will need to get a professional finish.

- Make-up sponge - *natural wedge shaped ones*
- Powder brush - *large soft (preferably sable)*
- Blusher brush - *slightly smaller that powder brush*
- Eye shadow brush - *soft tip, rounded brush*
- Eye shadow sponge - *sponge top applicator*
- Eyelash brush/comb combo - *course hair with plastic comb*
- Lip brush - *retractable with cover preferred*
- Eyelash curlers - *choose a professional quality curler*

ABOUT

Gillian Armour Image Consulting Fact Sheet

Headquarters: San Francisco, California

Telephone: (415)536-3111

www.GillianArmour.com (image tools, courses and seminars)

www.ImageTalks.com (ready-made seminars for trainers)

www.FashionImageInstitute.com (online fashion, image and style e-courses)

Since 2001, Gillian Armour Image Consulting, helmed by Gillian Armour, has helped men and women with their appearance, self-esteem, wardrobe, grooming and body language in ways that empower them to change.

Armour's background in fashion for companies like Macy's, I. Magnin and Jessica McClintock led her to open a full-service image consultancy to provide everything from simple makeovers to complex image overhauls as well as workshops and classes for clients and those who wish to pursue a career as an image consultant. Her San Francisco studio includes a fashion library, hair and makeup areas, and a color and style analysis space.

She is certified by and a member of the Association of Image Consultants International (AICI). Clients include government, corporate and non-profit clients, as well as Fortune 500 Companies. Her extensive use of cutting edge technology allows her to consult in person and remotely, as well as teach classes and train image consultants in the U.S. and abroad from her headquarters in San Francisco.

Armour has published several books about fashion, color and body type, and has just completed a how-to guide to becoming an image consultant. In 2007, she formed Best Dressed^{sm} to help men, women and teens from economically challenged backgrounds enter the workforce by offering free of charge makeover and wardrobe services to qualified clients actively seeking employment. Best Dressed^{sm} is a 501(c) 3 nonprofit organization.

Associations and Certifications

- Certified Image Professional, Association of Image Consultants
- Certified Lumina® Color Analysis Professional, Donna Fujii Color
- Certified Professional Fashion Stylist and Personal Shopper, Fashion Image Institute
- Certified Personal Trainer, Circuit Training Instructor, Group Fitness and EZ8 Running Coach (NESTA)
- Certified in Sports Nutrition from American Sport and Fitness Association (ASFA)
- Professional Member - National Speakers Association (NSA)

WORKSHOPS

HOW TO GET THE MOST FROM YOUR EXISTING WARDROBE

Your budget tells you that you cannot afford another thing, and besides, your closet is already full of great clothes to wear. So what if some are last year's styles? Find out how you can update those styles. Learn to look at your existing clothing collection with newer, fresher eyes. Together we review the latest trends in fashion and show you how to match them with what you already may own. Discover how to tailor or change the cut of a jacket, pants, or top to make it more relevant to today's styling.

- How to coordinate your clothes and have more to wear.
- How many ways can you wear a white shirt? Sound like a trick question? The answer is – as many ways as you can think of.
- Learn how to think about your wardrobe basics this way and how doing so will increase your options for what to wear.
- Together we plan with spreadsheets how you can take that white shirt and add color via accessories and jewelry to create a bigger, better selection.
- Workbook shows you how to coordinate by using the color wheel and color rules thereby increasing your menu of wearable choices.

BARGAIN AND BUDGET SHOPPING

Everybody knows that bargain shopping in department stores these days is like having the cherry on the cake – it's so easy to find sale items and bargains. But let's not overlook the smaller stores and the antique collectives. Even the big box retailers offer quality and stylish fashion at great prices. In this group class you will learn:

- How to think outside the box of your traditional shopping patterns to find chic, unique fashion choices.
- To plan for your purchases instead of just hunting for the latest, greatest and cheapest.
- What it takes to be fashion savvy and bargain happy when the choices are mind-boggling.

- How not to fall victim to fads and trends that cost you more (disposable fashion).
- To look for inexpensive (but quality) options for your working wardrobe.

MEND, SEW, TAILOR, AND RE-FASHION YOUR WAY TO STYLE

Back in the day when we had money to burn most of us threw out or donated clothes that had rips, holes or stains. We wasted a lot of money and some really great fashion. It's time to be green about your clothing inventory. In this informative and fun class you will learn to:

- Edit and process the clothes in your closet that need some TLC.
- Take another look at styles that no longer fit you and discover how to make them work.
- Create brand new styles from some of your old classics.
- Work with your tailor to shorten, lengthen, widen or shrink those clothes you have long sidelined.
- Let go the emotional hold you have on favorite styles that really no longer fit, flatter, or shape you.

I NEVER DRY CLEAN – HOW I SAVED MYSELF $1250 IN ONE YEAR!

My mother was a great innovator and creative thinker. She had to come up with solutions to the enormous expenses of managing a family of ten people! I learned many cost-cutting methods from her especially when it came to taking care of clothes. We can all benefit from a mother's wisdom in this fashion boot camp class! You will discover how:

- To save a lot of money just by using the "hand wash" cycle of your washing machine.
- Discover why "Dry Clean Only" clothes are marked that way.
- Which fabrics really are "Dry Clean Only".
- Home dry cleaning kits – what they can and cannot do.
- What about difficult stains?

SHOW ME THE FASHION – CREATING A 15 PIECE WORKING WARDROBE FOR UNDER $500

Sound impossible? Not in my book. As a professional shopper it's my job to work within the budget limitations of my clients so I have learnt to shop at all levels of a fashion budget. Find out that you don't have to limit your budget shopping to department and specialty shops.

- Discover how to catalog shop, planning coordinates as you peruse your options.
- Discover how to hunt and pick from the sales racks for "bang for buck" merchandise.
- Plan a 15 piece wardrobe graph to mix-n-match and extend your wearable choices.
- Choose accessories that upgrade, embellish, and extend plain looks.
- Put your personal spin on classic sportswear and look like a million.

DIY – HAIR, NAILS AND FACIALS AND SAVE $$$

Here's a challenge for you fashionistas out there – make a list of how much you spend every month on pedicures, manicures, haircuts, colors and facials. That's the money you could save by doing-it-yourself (DIY). As they say, "a penny saved is a penny earned," so what better way to save a few than to learn how to pamper yourself? During this class you will discover:

- How to find great prices on beauty services and supplies.
- Discount salons – the good, the bad and the one's to avoid.
- Beauty schools – how to pick and choose from their menus.
- Gratis products and samples – learn how to ask for these freebies.
- Where to get your makeup done – for FREE.

YOUR CLOSET IS FULL OF SURPRISES – 10 WAYS TO GET MORE STYLE FROM EXISTING CLOTHING PIECES

Do you find yourself in a clothing rut with nothing exciting to wear? Do you tend to wear the same favorite pieces over and over again, rarely mixing it up? There is good news – discover the surprises your closet will yield AFTER you have emptied it completely. This fun workshop introduces you to the idea of radical change and re-invention, plus:

- How purging your closet leads to re-inventing a whole new wardrobe.
- Find long lost favorites in your closet and put them to good use.
- Get rid of the un-wearables, the un-bearables and the un-desireables.
- Plan a dress-up day with best friends and re-discover what you love about your clothes.
- How throwing a "Girlfriend's Closet Party" will release your attachment to old clothes.

THE IMPORTANCE OF FEELING GOOD IN YOUR CLOTHES

Do the clothes you wear make you feel frumpy and dumpy or confident and beautiful? Is the way you dress telling the world who you really are? Do you dress to impress others and forsake how you feel in your own clothes?

- Discover your "style personality" and how it reveals itself through your clothing and accessory choices.
- Take the Style Personality Quiz and get the answers to looking and feeling better.
- Discover a style that is uniquely you, that gives you a greater sense of self.
- Explore options for dressing to a changing body.
- Make impressions about you that count.

IMAGE SERVICES

Research has shown that a poor image can be professionally costly as well as personally painful. Both individuals and companies can experience tremendous benefits by improving their image. That's why a growing number of people are turning to professional image consultants.

"Today, image professionals are beginning to be on the same level as Interior designers. Anyone who wants to look their best and be appropriate will now hire an image consultant." Anna Soo Wildermuth, AICI President.

As a professional *and* certified international image consultant, I specialize in visual appearance and non-verbal communication. I counsel individual and corporate clients on appearance, behavior, and communication skills through individual consultations, coaching, presentations, seminars and workshops. My Image Consultancy is not about a radical makeover or plastic surgery: it is about helping you with your appearance, wardrobe, grooming, and body language in a way that empowers you to change.

My company, Gillian Armour Image Consulting, is allied with other trained and certified experts from image related fields. Together we work with you to custom tailor a complete image package for all your appearance needs. From a simple makeover to complex visual branding consultations, the following is a list of services we offer that are geared toward helping you achieve your maximum potential as a well dressed person.

- Image in Business
- Visual Branding
- Image Analysis
- Image for Men
- Body/Shape Analysis
- On Line Analysis Programs
- Wardrobe Edit/ Closet Organizing
- Custom Color Analysis
- Makeup Consultation
- Etiquette
- Non-Verbal Communication Consultation
- Personal Shopping

- Personal Style interview
- Appearance Evaluation
- Body Shape, Fit and Sizing
- Evaluation of Non-Verbal Communication
- Evaluation of Communication Skills
- Style Collage and Core Wardrobe Workbook
- Shopping Preferences and Plans
- What is Image?
- What Does it Take to be Successful?
- Basic Professional Wardrobe Capsule
- Purchase Planning
- Sample Wardrobe with Pictures (5 outfits on mannequin)
- Wardrobe Hints
- Wardrobe Planning
- Investment Dressing
- Image Checklist
- Fabric Information
- Eyewear Guide
- The Job Interview
- Dating Attire Do's and Don'ts
- Head shot/Portrait Planning
- Fashion Styling

BOOKS BY GILLIAN ARMOUR

- Mastering the Art of Dressing Well
- The Fashion Stylist
- Bridal Stylist - Consulting for Brides and Weddings
- Mastering the Art of Business Image
- Mastering the Art of Image Consulting
- Glamour Girls Guide to Looking Gorgeous
- How to Dress Guide - Asian Body
- Reigning Over Closet Chaos
- Are You Coordinated?
- Ten Steps to Absolute Chic
- How to Do an Image Consult
- Social Media Marketing for Image Consultants
- How to Write and Produce an E-Book
- What's Your Style Personality?

PRODUCTS @ www.gillianarmour.com

- Color Season Makeup
- Custom Color Analysis
- Color Season Guides
- Body Shape Guides
- Royalty Free jpeg's for Fashion Coordination
- Licensing program "My Style Firm" for certified fashion stylists and image consultants
- E-courses
- E-books

Gillian Armour, AICI CIP

Image Consultant /Celebrity Stylist and fashion columnist for *Sage Magazine*. Gillian appeared for several seasons on the award winning NBC show *"Dream Makeover Hawaii"* as its official image consultant and stylist.

As a Style Director Gillian has produced fashion shows, photography shoots, TV commercials and TV Movies. She has styled many celebrities and teaches a certified course for budding Fashion Stylists. Gillian takes pride in being the pioneering creator of on-line Image, Style and Fashion e-learning courses. She continues to expand the image industry by certifying students globally.

Her career in retail fashion reaches back 25 years and includes executive, managerial and buying positions with retailers *Macy's, I. Magnin* and *House of Fraser*, London.

Gillian is the author of many eBooks on image and writes for successful fashion social networking sites. Gillian was recently named a beauty expert for several high fashion magazines and blogs about fashion, style and image frequently.

Contact: 1-415-230-0015

www.GillianArmour.com
www.FashionImageInstitute.com

NOTES

Made in the USA
Lexington, KY
28 May 2012